Original title:
Sweet as Grapes

Copyright © 2025 Creative Arts Management OÜ
All rights reserved.

Author: Henry Beaumont
ISBN HARDBACK: 978-1-80586-258-1
ISBN PAPERBACK: 978-1-80586-730-2

Savoring Sunset Stains

A splash of purple on my face,
Trying to catch the fruity trace.
Like a raccoon with sticky paws,
I dance around without a cause.

The twilight giggles, off it goes,
As my shirt now sports a new prose.
What once was dinner, now a mess,
But oh, this joy, I must confess!

Cradled in Nature's Lap

I sit among the leafy vines,
Whispers of laughter, nature shines.
A grape rolls past, it's on the run,
Chasing it down could be real fun.

The ground is soft, my laugh is loud,
While critters gaze from leafy shrouds.
My plump friends pop with silly glee,
Nature's blanket, just you and me!

Frolic Among the Vines

Oh, what a riot, rolling grapes,
With all their squish, they make escapes.
Chasing laughter in the sunny glow,
Silly antics make the good times flow.

A bouncing ball of purple bliss,
Who knew that fruit could be such this?
With every stomp, they squirt and shine,
Guess it's just another grape-y time!

Sun-Kissed Elixirs

In the jug of joy, they dance and sway,
A fizzy spectacle, come what may.
With bubbly laughter in each sip,
Every taste brings a little trip.

Friends gather 'round, the glasses clink,
With every gulp, we start to think.
What's life without a twisty cheer?
Let's sip the sunshine, spread the cheer!

Shadows in the Grape Leaves

In the garden of chuckles, shadows play,
Grape leaves giggle, dancing all day.
Sipping sunshine, what a delight,
Jesters in nature, a whimsical sight.

Bees in tuxedos buzz past my ear,
They toast to the harvest, it's all very clear.
With a wink and a nudge, they start a parade,
Nature's own comedy, perfectly made.

Lively Harvest Echoes

In vineyards bright, laughter does soar,
Bunches of laughter, who could ask for more?
Buckets of giggles, rolling downhill,
A prankster's paradise, with laughter to spill.

Old vines chuckle, sharing their tales,
Of mischievous raccoons raiding their trails.
A banquet of joy as we pick and we pluck,
With every grape harvested, more giggles struck.

The Aroma of Bliss

Sniffing the air, I feel quite elated,
The scent of joy, highly rated.
Fruity perfumes, teasing my nose,
With every whiff, a smile just grows.

Clusters of laughter, bursting in cheer,
Each grape's a joke, whispered so near.
I trip on the vines, and tumble with glee,
In this juicy realm, I'm wild and free.

Flinging Blossoms in the Breeze

Petals are flung like confetti in space,
Grape bloom parties, a laughable race.
I swipe at the blossoms, they dance in the air,
A game of tag, with fun everywhere.

Swirling in circles, we twirl with delight,
Breezes are giggling, oh what a sight!
With every sip of nature's good cheer,
Life bursts into laughter, the harvest is near.

Bunches of Joy

In a garden where giggles bloom,
Tiny critters dance, dispel the gloom.
With every vine, a chuckle grows,
Tickled leaves in sunlit shows.

Bouncing berries, what a sight,
They roll on hills, pure delight.
Slippery laughs as they take a dive,
Who knew fruit could bring such jive?

Juicy jests in every bite,
One squished and sparks take flight.
They whisper secrets, so absurd,
Even the squirrels stop and heard.

So grab a handful, have a taste,
In this comedy, none go to waste.
With laughter they fill, both young and old,
Like tales of joy, forever told.

A Tapestry of Sweets

A patchwork quilt of fruity fun,
Giggles sparkle, just like the sun.
Each piece a story, woven tight,
With fruity flavors, pure delight.

A berry bold with a cheeky grin,
It tickles your tongue, let the fun begin.
Plucked from bushes topped with glee,
In this patch, we're all so free.

When sunsets glow on grapevine trails,
The air is thick with fruity tales.
With every nibble, laughter blooms,
Joy spills over like fuzzy fumes.

So come on down, join the spree,
Where fruits and laughter dance with glee.
Each slice of whimsy, a burst of cheer,
In this tapestry, we'll disappear.

Luscious Labyrinth

In a maze of flavors, the giggles flow,
Sticky fingers, racing toes.
Round the corner, what's this mess?
A fruit-filled crash, oh what a jest!

Berries bounce like playful sprites,
Whispering jokes through moonlit nights.
Chasing down a runaway pear,
Laughter echoes through the air.

Winding paths of juicy cheer,
Every turn brings giggles near.
A mishap here, a squish over there,
This maze of merriment, beyond compare.

So wander through this silly spree,
With every bite, you'll dance with glee.
Fall down, laugh, get up once more,
In this labyrinth, joy's in store!

Fields of Fruitful Wonder

In the fields where flavors play,
Bouncing fruits lead the way.
With every stomp, the laughter swells,
In a world where fun just dwells.

Cherries giggle, apples wink,
They spark a smile quicker than you think.
Rolling down the grassy slope,
A fruity parade, we laugh and hope.

Bees buzzing jokes like quirky friends,
Sharing sweetness that never ends.
With sticky hands and joyful hearts,
In fruit-filled fields, fun never departs.

So grab a bushel, take a seat,
Where laughter and fruit continuously meet.
In these fruitful meadows bright and gay,
Let's celebrate each giggly day!

The Tapestry of Taste

In the orchard, laughter sways,
Chasing sunbeams on their ways.
Fruitful pranks from vine to vine,
Tickle tongues like diluted wine.

Jesters dance in green attire,
Chucking grapes like small live fire.
Falling down with fruity glee,
A harvest of hilarity.

Lush Reveries

Under heavy canopies,
We're told jokes by buzzing bees.
Each grape hides a giggle shrill,
Sipping joy with every thrill.

Leaping lizards join the fun,
Snap! A grape, and on the run!
Witty fruits roll down the hill,
With a punchline, get your fill!

Casks of Daydreams

Barrels filled with laughter's brew,
Jesting spirits, oh so true.
Whimsical treads in the yard,
Where every grape sings the bard.

Wobbly feet on grassy floors,
Ricocheting off vineyard doors.
In this cask of joy, we play,
And sip the night away!

A Palette of Pleasures

Colors splash like grand confetti,
Fruits turn jokes into confetti.
Bananas slip on puns so bright,
Kiwi's wink brings sheer delight.

Juggling berries, round and round,
With juicy giggles all around.
To taste the fun, we take a bite,
In this palette, life feels light.

Trysts Beneath the Vines

Two lovers giggle, grape juice in hand,
They stumble and tumble, oh isn't life grand?
A cluster of laughs, they wrestle and play,
While birds chirp a tune in their own funny way.

Fingers are sticky, the sun's blazing bright,
They dance in the vineyard, oh what a sight!
A fox sneaks a peek, then runs off in fright,
As our lovers continue this cheeky delight.

Lush Afternoon Delights

In a field full of pearls, they picnic on grass,
With wine and some cheese, they toast—and they pass!
A raccoon joins, curious, sneaking a bite,
While laughter erupts, oh what a delight!

Their voices echo, floating up in the air,
As ants march in rhythm, no worry or care.
A squirrel steals crumbs, making off with a cheer,
They cheer him on, through giggles and beer.

The Essence of Rural Joy

Underneath the sun, the fields sway and bend,
A goat in a hat, what a sight to commend!
They toss him a snack, he nibbles with flair,
While laughter erupts like it's free everywhere.

Bubbles in barrels, they splash and they pop,
The neighbors all laugh, they can't seem to stop.
A pig in a bowtie joins in on the fun,
His odd little dance steals the show, everyone!

Memory Lane in Grape Domain

Old friends reminisce, with glasses held high,
They toast to the days flying swiftly on by.
A dog steals a cork, running off with a grin,
Leads their chase through the vines, oh where to begin?

With snippets of joy, and tales filled with cheer,
They spin round in circles, the end is unclear.
A cat on a fence looks down with a glare,
As if to say, 'Come on, life's meant to share!'

Bubble of Joy

In a glass all frothy and bright,
Bubbles dance with sheer delight.
Laughter spills from every sip,
Joyful hops, no need to trip.

Bubbling hiccups, cheery and loud,
Riding waves, we dance in a crowd.
Let's toast to feelings that delight,
Sparkling fun shines day and night.

Rippled Silver Clusters

Clusters glisten, shining gold,
We giggle at silly tales told.
Pop a berry, taste a dream,
Slapstick moments, laughter's beam.

Fizzy pop and fruity cheers,
We toast again, dismissing fears.
Wobble and giggle, sunny plays,
Life's a circus in berry days.

Summer Casanova

Flirting with sunshine, what a sight,
A juicy charmer, oh so bright.
With a wink and cheesy grin,
Berries blush, let the games begin.

Sipping juice, we're feeling grand,
Laughter bubbles, hand in hand.
Bio-breaks in the shade, not a care,
In our fruity love, no one dare.

Tangy Romance

In a picnic basket, love is found,
Tangy whispers make hearts pound.
Dancing taste buds, flavors collide,
In this merry feast, we take pride.

Sharing slices, laughter shared,
Jokes like syrup, no one's scared.
With every bite, we roll and sway,
In this tangy dance, let's play.

The Dance of the Vine

In a garden where laughter grows,
The vines twirl, striking silly poses.
Leaves wiggle in a comical way,
As the sun chuckles throughout the day.

Bunches jive while the breezes blow,
They've got rhythm, putting on a show.
In their party pants, they sway and spin,
Inviting all critters to join in.

Slippery squirrel joins with a grin,
Attempting to dance, but he tumbles in.
The ants march by, in perfect line,
Sipping on dew, they think they're divine.

With twinkling roots and playful sprout,
These viney folks wear laughter, no doubt.
As daylight fades and stars appear,
The grapes giggle loud, spreading cheer!

Savoring the Sun

Bright rays tickle the morning leaves,
Grape-clad jokers play tricks, like thieves.
They bask in glory, wearing shades,
As beetles roll dice beneath the glades.

A snail in shades, he struts with flair,
Races a beetle to see who's where.
With every step, they chuckle and chime,
As shadows dance in this grinning rhyme.

Buzzing bees join the grape's parade,
With tiny hats, they're not afraid.
The sun spills laughter, a golden stream,
Every plant knows this isn't a dream.

In a world where giggles are number one,
The grapes all toast to a job well done.
With rosy cheeks, they bask till night,
Laughing together, it feels so right!

Tangled in Bliss

Vines intertwine, a playground of fun,
Snuggling 'neath rays, each basking one.
With a hiccup of joy, they sway and play,
Ripe laughter drips like juice on a tray.

A squirrel swings low, then high he flies,
Landing in a bunch, to everyone's surprise.
He steals a grape, in a peek-a-boo game,
While others giggle and call out his name.

Dance partners spin, in a joyous knot,
Stumbling and tumbling, giggling a lot.
They tumble down, rolling on the ground,
A grape-tastic mess, the best fun around.

Under a blanket of shimmering stars,
The giggles echo, a chorus from afar.
Tangled together, in love and in jest,
The grape brigade knows they're truly blessed!

From Earth to Elixir

In the soil's embrace, they dream and scheme,
Transforming wishes into zesty cream.
With every drop of dew, they sing,
About sipping joy and the laughter it brings.

As the blender whirls, they scream with glee,
"Let's mix it up, come party with me!"
With a splash and a giggle, they're suddenly bright,
Potions of chuckles that dance in the light.

On table tops, the goblets clink,
Sticky mustaches form as people wink.
Each sip bursting with a cheeky grin,
While folks toast to the silliness within.

From earth to drink, it's a bumpy ride,
But oh the fun when you toss aside pride.
Together they giggle, ensure no one slips,
To laugh loudly over the grape-flavored sips!

Grapevine Murmurs

In a bunch they giggle and sway,
Plump and round, just ready to play.
They whisper secrets, oh so bold,
Under sun rays, their stories unfold.

A grape slipped out, took a quick spin,
Bouncing around, with a cheeky grin.
"Catch me if you can!" it cried in delight,
Rolling down hills, a comical flight.

Another one shouted from its vine,
"Life is too short, let's sip some wine!"
A hiccup, a tumble, then laughter in air,
These fruity revelers, debonair and rare.

Harvest time's near, the party's full swing,
Dancing around, they're the grape kings and queens.
With jests and joy, they frolic and tease,
Making the orchard feel like a breeze.

Threads of Nature's Wonders

Oh, little spheres in a leafy green dance,
With the bees buzzing by, they prance.
Hanging on vines, like jewels they twirl,
In the sun's warm glow, they give it a whirl.

"Who knew being fruit could be such a thrill?"
Said one to another, with a juicy chill.
"From vineyard to glass, what an exciting ride,"
They chuckled and giggled, in sheer grape pride.

Every plump one dreams of a splashy fate,
"A party, a picnic, hey, don't make me wait!"
They fashion themselves into luscious designs,
Feeling quite grand, like the finest of wines.

As sunset paints skies, they raucously cheer,
"With love and laughter, let's toast the year!"
Oh, the tales that these tiny fruits could share,
In threads of nature's wonders, laughter fills the air.

Vineyards in Twilight

Amidst the vines, where shadows play,
A troupe of grapes scheme night and day.
With twinkling lights and stars align,
They plot their pranks, oh so divine.

"Let's roll downhill, end up in a bowl,
Let the farmers find us, they'll lose control!"
A cascade of giggles erupts from the crew,
As they tumble and roll, like they've something to prove.

The moon rises high, like a custard pie,
"Now watch us, dear moon, we'll give it a try!"
In a bottle they dream, with a splash and a pop,
Bubbling with joy, they'll never stop.

With the twilight embracing the verdant land,
Grapeful concoctions, they make quite a stand.
Under the stars, they're free like a breeze,
In vineyards at twilight, they dance with ease.

Moonlit Harvest Ballads

Gather round, little grapes on the vine,
Under moonlit skies, you'll surely shine.
A night of music, laughter, and glee,
Join the ballad of the fruity spree!

"Sing a tune of the sweetest surprise,
With a plump little jump and glittering eyes!"
From vine to table, a giggling chase,
Each one convinced they'll win the race.

As the harvest moon shines with envy so bold,
They squish and squash, making stories unfold.
With each burst of flavor, a chuckle erupts,
Nature's own jesters, the fun never stops.

So toast to the grapes, in their moonlit spree,
With laughter and joy, come dance with me!
For every plush globule, a story untold,
In moonlit harvest ballads, life's treasures unfold.

Harvest Moon Serenade

Under the moon, we dance with glee,
Grapes in hand, as silly as can be.
A squish here, a splash there, oh my,
We laugh and toast to wine gone awry!

In the fields we prance like clowns,
With purple stains that match our crowns.
Who knew these fruits held such delight,
As we stomp and trip into the night!

Cheese and crackers, a feast set wide,
A grape-squeezed soda, what a ride!
We chuckle at our fruity fate,
With juice on hands, it's grape-tastic fate!

Beneath the stars, our laughter soars,
As hiccups echo from our pours.
To harvest nights, we raise a cheer,
With silly tales, we'll drink the year!

Luscious Bunches of Delight

Bunches hung like chandeliers,
We pick and munch, forgetting fears.
Our fingers sticky, faces bright,
A grape war starts, oh what a sight!

With each toss, laughter fills the air,
Friendships grow with every pear.
Not a care for stains or fuss,
Just grape juice laughter, sheer plus!

Oh dear, what's this? A grape-tastrophe!
I slipped and fell, who knew they'd flee!
Watch them roll, oh what a chase,
Grapes on the run, a comical race!

In the end, we sit and sigh,
With giggles echoing, oh so spry.
Life's a party with these fruity bites,
In our little world of grape-filled nights!

Tasting the Sunlit Orchards

In orchards bright, we taste the fun,
With sun-kissed grapes, we've just begun.
We click our heels and toss a few,
As juice drips down, we laugh anew!

A picnic set with snacks galore,
We munch on grapes, then want some more.
"Is it lunch or are we just playing?"
In the grape parade, there's no delaying!

With our hats flopping, we spin around,
Silly dances on grassy ground.
A grape-themed conga 'round the tree,
Sweet grapes for fun and jubilee!

As the sun dips low, we gather near,
Sharing tales with a popsicle cheer.
Embracing silliness, our hearts will soar,
In sunlit orchards, we'll laugh for more!

Whispers of the Vineyard

In the vineyard, whispers float,
As silly ghosts in gowns we wrote.
Grapes giggle as we chase and peek,
Laughter echoes, it's laughter we seek!

Stomping grapes with shoes so tall,
"I hope I don't drop, or slip and fall!"
A grape splat here, a berry boo,
We're planting joy with each gooey goo!

Hoop skirts twirl and baskets sway,
We juggle grapes in a clumsy ballet.
With every toss, a sigh and roar,
Vines chuckle back, wanting more!

When night descends, we raise our cup,
To all the grapes who filled us up.
With a grin and a sip, we'll always claim,
In the vineyard's heart, there's laughter's name!

Fortunes of Clusters

In the orchard, grapes dress so fine,
Rumor has it they sip on wine.
Clustered secrets, each one a tease,
Telling tales with the rustle of leaves.

Juggling fruits is quite the art,
A grape rolled off—oh, where'd it depart?
Laughter echoes, as they take a spin,
Chasing the berries, we lose and win.

Mischief lurks in the vine's embrace,
Sipping juice, we fall from grace.
Drowsy bees with a polka-dot suit,
Stand guard at the entrance, really quite cute!

Yet every cluster has its tale,
Of juice spilled wide on an old gray snail.
With giggles and glee, the fruits take flight,
Under the moon, they party all night!

Joy's Vineyard Vistas

Strolling through rows, a sight to behold,
Grapes gossip softly, their stories unfold.
Ripe and round, they wiggle with cheer,
Each bunch a jest, full of joy and beer.

The sun beams in like a teasing dancer,
A grape in a top hat—what a romancer!
Bouncing around, they spread their delight,
Who knew a vineyard could tickle so right?

Pixies frolic, sipping dew drops,
Grapes in a party with wobbly hops.
A truce in the field, no more rival schemes,
Just laughter and whispers of soda pop dreams.

In the twilight glow, the moon starts to grin,
As grapes make a pact for a dance-off win.
With little red shoes, they shuffle and jive,
Life is a party—oh, how we thrive!

Dancing with the Orchard Spirits

In the orchard's dance, the fruits are the stars,
Twisting and swirling, they flirt with the jars.
With laughter as bubbles, they pop all around,
While giggly spirits join in with a sound.

A grape lost its hat, oh what a sight!
Dancing around in the warm summer light.
With a wink and a nod, the pears strike a pose,
And the plump little plums put on fancy clothes.

Spirits are buzzing, and the apples are bold,
Telling grand tales of the harvest of old.
"Let's juggle the fruits!" cries a cheeky young berry,
Playing hopscotch with laughter, it's all so merry!

In every spin, a giggle erased,
As the fruits compete for best harvest taste.
In this orchard of joy, where friends never part,
We sip the fun life from a grape that's smart!

A Brush with Sweetness

In a garden bright with cheer,
A bunch of laughs is growing near.
With every munch, I giggle loud,
Become a grape, I feel so proud!

Rolling down this sunny lane,
I'm stuck inside a juicy grain.
With friends to share this silly spree,
We'll laugh till fruit flies cover me!

Those purple spheres from nature's bin,
Give hugs with every little grin.
A pinball of delight and glee,
I'll bounce around like ants at tea!

So here's to snacks so plump and round,
My fruity pals, they're always found.
In every bite, joy finds its way,
Let's giggle with our grub today!

The Lure of Juicy Pursuits

In search of snack, I roam the street,
Chasing dreams on little feet.
A vine that whispers, "Come and play!"
I'll leap right in without delay!

Bouncing off the bumpy ground,
A carousel of fun I've found.
With every squish, a burst, a cheer,
These tangy gems, oh dear, oh dear!

Silly faces, juice will fly,
Sticky hands, oh my, oh my!
With laughter blooming all around,
These zany fruits will keep me bound!

A race to gobble, who can win?
We'll snack and joke, it's such a sin!
Just watch out for the seeds that sprout,
They're plotting on a juicy shout!

Timeless Bounty

A bowl of fun, it sits so grand,
With hidden treasures close at hand.
Each squishy bite, a fountain flows,
And all my worries go like crows!

A fruit-filled game of peekaboo,
The giggles dance, it's all so true.
With purple jewels all on display,
I dare to munch, come what may!

From vine to mouth, a playful chase,
These chewy bombs bring smiles and grace.
They burst with laughter, one by one,
Life's simple joys—oh, isn't it fun?

So gather 'round and take a seat,
Join in the laughter, oh what a treat!
We'll savor moments, wild, not shy,
Let's toast to life as grapes roll by!

A Toast to Sunlit Days

Under sunbeams, bright and warm,
A juicy gang begins to swarm.
With silly jokes that make me grin,
Their antics cause my head to spin!

Hopping high, the flavors fly,
A fruity circus, oh my, oh my!
We juggle laughs and toss the fun,
With every squeeze, the day's begun!

The laughter bubbles, bounces high,
When grapes unite, they touch the sky.
Sweet and tangy, they keep me giddy,
These fruit-filled pranks, they're oh-so-witty!

Raise a glass to precious times,
Grapes and giggles in sweet chimes.
Let's dance and munch, come what may,
Together, we'll savor the sunlit day!

Sugar-Coated Whimsy

In the garden, giggles grow,
With fruit that swings and sways just so.
Bouncing berries, round and bright,
Whispering secrets under moonlight.

Bees do a jig, oh what a sight,
As they buzz around, full of delight.
Their dance a riddle, their flight a game,
While I ponder if they taste the same.

Oh, the plump ones boast, so soft and round,
While others tumble off the ground.
If laughter's fruit, then pass the bowl,
Let's feast on fun, that's our goal!

So grab a grape, don't be in haste,
Each nibble's a giggle, life's a sweet taste.
With every pop, a new punchline,
In this fruity circus, all is divine!

The Aroma of Nature's Heart

In vineyards lush, the scents collide,
Grapes snicker as they take a ride.
They twirl and bounce, so full of cheer,
Whispering tales for all to hear.

A wobbly squirrel joins the feast,
Wearing his hat—a grape-lover's beast!
He cracks a joke, the raccoons cringe,
As they do the grapevine shuffle, on the fringe.

The sunbeam giggles, tickling leaves,
As we pluck juicy treasures with ease.
"Have a taste!" the fruit seems to cheer,
Everyone laughs, "We're all grape here!"

So let's raise a toast, with juice galore,
To nature's laughter that we adore.
With every sip, we'll sing a song,
In this playful world, where we belong!

Nature's Liquid Joy

From lush green vines, the nectar flows,
A splash of sunshine, nobody knows.
Sipping bubbly bliss from the vine,
Life's a party, oh how divine!

Grape juice juggles in tiny cups,
As we twirl like twinkling fireflies in ups.
Each sip a giggle, each gulp a grin,
We dance and laugh—let the fun begin!

The little ladybugs tap their feet,
On sugary paths, they dance and greet.
Those fruity wonders, a wild brigade,
In this juicy tale, joy is made.

So drink up, pals, here's a toast (cheers!),
To clinking glasses and grape-scented cheers.
In liquid joy, we find our muse,
Let's laugh and sip, it's ours to use!

Hues of Unfurling Joy

In twilight's glow, the colors burst,
A festival of hues—oh, how we thirst!
Purples and greens in a tangled spree,
Nature's palette, a wild jubilee.

Here comes a grape wearing a crown,
Bouncing around in a dazzling gown.
"Catch me if you can!" it sings in jest,
While cherries giggle, "We're the best!"

The apples chime in with a squeaky sound,
Declaring their worth, they roll around.
But the jolly grapes, with their cheeky glow,
Just laugh and dance, stealing the show.

So let's paint the night with all our fun,
In every grape-sparked laugh, we're one.
As colors blend and laughter plays,
In this fruity world, joy stays!

Vineyards of Memory

In the vineyard where we play,
Laughter rolls in a light ballet.
We'll stomp the grapes and dance in glee,
Making juice as sticky as can be.

The sun sets low, the shadows grow,
We trip on vines, just so you know.
Slip, slide, and take a spill,
Giggles echo, we've had our fill.

Uncle Joe claims he can sip,
A glass so big, it's like a ship.
He spills a drop, it catches light,
We laugh so hard, it's pure delight.

Each bottle tells a tale or two,
Of pranks we pulled and our silly crew.
With every sip, we recall the spree,
In this silly world where wild minds roam free.

Twilight in the Orchard

Underneath the twilight sky,
Fruit hangs low, and so do I.
With branches bowing, all aglow,
We start our feast, but fate won't slow.

Cousin Tim has quite the aim,
He throws a fruit, oh what a game!
It bounces back and hits him square,
He laughs aloud, without a care.

Each bite a burst, a playful shout,
The orchard's laughter never doubts.
A round of juice, a sticky tide,
In this hilarious fruit-filled ride.

So if you wander where we roam,
Watch your head or you'll become foam,
Grabbing grapes that take to flight,
In this orchard of joyous fright.

Juice Dripping from the Vine

The grapes above begin to sway,
As if they're dancing, come what may.
With each plump orb, a silly wish,
To catch our dreams, a juicy swish.

A puddle forms, a grape juice sea,
We paddle boats made of debris.
Oh look, it seems the dog just fell,
Into the mix, now that's a smell!

Uncle Bob thinks he's a chef,
Creates a feast from all the mess.
"Just drink it quick!" he claims with pride,
But slippery paths soon prove the ride.

A running race, we take the lead,
Juice stains our shirts, it's all we need.
In the vineyard's heart, we jump and scream,
Living our funny, fruity dream.

Nectar's Embrace

There's nectar dripping from the vine,
Taste it quick, it's simply divine.
But watch your step, the ground is wet,
One slip now, and you'll regret!

A bee buzzes past, oh what a thrill,
Chasing us while we stand so still.
It's gone, thank goodness, we can resume,
And sip the nectar, spread the bloom.

Slathered in juice from head to toe,
We claim to be the juiciest show.
With sticky fingers and laughter loud,
We're the silliest, right, and proud!

As night falls soft, and stars are near,
We toast to fun, let's raise a cheer.
In this embrace, we're free to play,
In our orchard where we laugh all day!

Velvet Hues of Fall

Leaves tumble down like clumsy fools,
In colors bright, they break the rules.
Fleeting moments dance in the air,
Nature's chuckle, without a care.

Squirrels scurry, looking for nuts,
With comedy in their little struts.
They hoard away their fall delight,
As if they'll laugh all winter night.

Pumpkins frolic, losing their round,
Rolling away with a silly sound.
Autumn's giggles echo all around,
As the harvest moon shares its crown.

So let us play in this golden hue,
Laughing with trees, the sky so blue.
For in this season, joy does bloom,
In velvet tones, we whittle gloom.

Dining with the Sun

A picnic planned beneath the rays,
A feast of fruits for sunny days.
Lemons and limes join citrus cheer,
While ants audition to be quite near.

The sun spills laughter on our spread,
As squirrels nibble on crumbs of bread.
Juicy morsels drip and roll,
Getting messy is the goal!

Watermelon slices wear a grin,
Spitting seeds, oh, let the fun begin!
The sun sets slow, we wave goodbye,
As fireflies wink, and the stars sigh.

So let's delight in every bite,
With fruity laughter, hearts take flight.
Dining bliss beneath the sky,
Where fun and flavor always lie.

Enchanted Vineyard Tales

In vineyards lush, the grapes convene,
Whispering tales of the unseen.
They giggle and sway in the eve's embrace,
With juicy secrets, a merry race.

A waltz of wine in aging casks,
Even the barrels wear silly masks.
They clink and clatter in their stall,
As if to say, 'We're having a ball!'

The vines entwine with such finesse,
Telling jokes in hearty jest.
If pickers slip, the grapes all cheer,
For laughter credits, it will appear!

So raise a glass to this great affair,
To vines that giggle in the air.
In every sip, a story's spun,
With every laugh, our hearts are won.

Savoring the Orchard's Hues

In orchards wide, the apples gleam,
They bounce around like a joyful dream.
Cider flows as if on cue,
While pies declare, 'We're for you!'

Bumbling bees buzz, chase off the wasps,
With dainty dances, they take their hops.
A clownish fox the branches bounds,
As laughter rustles in the sounds.

A pumpkin patch dons hats of straw,
Playing dress-up without a flaw.
With every morsel kissed by the breeze,
The orchard giggles with grand ease.

So let us munch on nature's gifts,
In playful tones, our spirits lift.
For in this place of bountiful news,
We savor life's delightful hues.

The Lure of Ripeness

When they're plump and round, oh what a sight,
A snack so tempting, morning or night.
With juicy laughter spilling from each sphere,
One bite can have you grinning ear to ear.

On picnic blankets, they steal the show,
Their playful colors make the sun glow.
Just don't trip over baskets left in place,
Or you might end up with juice on your face!

The vine's a jungle where they dance and play,
A party of flavors, brightening the day.
As you munch away, do keep your eyes peeled,
For the neighbor's cat, who's stealthily healed!

So here's to the fruit that's nature's great prize,
With each little nibble, a giggle arises.
They boast of delight, with each little pop,
These cheeky delights, the fun just won't stop!

Nature's Candy

In a bowl, they sit with a glimmer and gleam,
A burst of fun, like a sugary dream.
Plucked from the vine, they laugh all the way,
Who knew nature had such a playful sway?

Chasing each other, they tumble and roll,
Making their case to steal every soul.
With roots in the ground but spirits so high,
Do they plan to take over? Oh my, oh my!

A joke in each bite, a giggle that pops,
Like they're having a party that never stops.
Forget the dessert that's heavy and dense,
These little orbs leave you laughing intense!

So gather around for a taste of the fun,
Nature's own treats, second to none.
As you munch with glee, and your worries disperse,
Remember the day just kept getting worse!

Fragrant Echoes

In orchards that sway with a fragrant delight,
These little gems dance; it's a whimsical sight.
They tickle your senses, with aromas so fine,
Like the air's full of giggles as they intertwine.

Each burst of flavor, a jester's parade,
With every soft nibble, a joke's perfectly made.
They whisper sweet secrets, as they tumble around,
In a comedic chaos, where laughter is found!

Add them to salads, or just munch on a few,
In a race 'gainst a squirrel who's much hipper than you.
With juice on your chin and a grin ear to ear,
These jolly escapers make memories clear.

So here's to the giggles, the joy that they bring,
With every bright taste, your heart starts to sing.
As laughter encircles, and friendships renew,
Nature's joke is ripe, come on, join the crew!

Gathered Delights

In a world of green, where the sun loves to peek,
These characters plump, and they're cheeky, not meek.
Gathered in bunches, they wiggle with glee,
Just waiting for someone to take them for tea.

You'll catch them grinning on a warm afternoon,
Claiming their stake, like a robust cartoon.
With every soft pop, they'll play a short song,
Reminding you, dear friend, you can't go wrong.

With colors so bright, they're like playful jesters,
Making each meal feel like a grand festival.
A comedy show where no one can miss,
Just don't let them fool you, or you'll end up in bliss!

So gather your crew for a fruity parade,
With laughter and crunch, let your worries fade.
These delightful treats will keep you up high,
In a world turned bright, you'll learn why and how why!

Nectar on the Breeze

Buzzing bees with a jiggle,
Skipping round like a figgle.
Drunk on nectar, they do dance,
Sipping life like it's romance.

Fruit flies flit without a care,
Making friends with pungent air.
They gather round the grape parade,
In sunshine warmth, they're all dismayed.

Bunches hanging, ripe and bold,
Jokes of juice, forever told.
They laugh and roll on tender vines,
Giggling in the sunny lines.

Underneath the leafy grow,
Chattering secrets, soft and low.
Nature's prank, a playful tease,
Sharing giggles on the breeze.

Ripe with Possibility

In a vineyard, dreams unfold,
Funny visions to behold.
Grapes in shades of purple gleam,
Sometimes they burst, it's quite a theme.

Wobbling on the vine, they strut,
Flashing hues like they're in a rut.
A grape that mutters, "Watch me shine!"
While others scream, "I'm out of line!"

Each plump orb, a silly tale,
One claims it's got a tiny whale.
Together in their juicy grind,
They share laughs and unwind their mind.

Wacky dances on the ground,
Where the laughter knows no bound.
With every crush, the giggles grow,
As they spin in the grape-tango.

Sunlit Harvest

Under sun, the grapes take flight,
Bouncing round, a funny sight.
Teasing leaves in gentle sway,
They plot shenanigans each day.

Reluctant vines hang their heads,
Claiming they need cozy beds.
But wait! Here comes the sunlit cheer,
"Time to party, grab some beer!"

Crimson blushes, golden hues,
Witty tales and playful moos.
As robins join the merry scene,
Chasing grapes and eating green.

In that warmth, joy's in abundance,
Mixing laughter with a fondness.
As clusters giggle, life's parade,
Underneath the sun, they've played.

The Color of Abundance

Round and plump, the colors shout,
Belly laughs and grape-filled clout.
A riot of hues in every bunch,
"Who stole my snack?" asks one with a crunch.

Grapes in groups, they like to boast,
"I'm juicier than that old roast!"
They squabble and jest beneath the vine,
Telling tales of their rich design.

Handsome green and purple pride,
In the breeze, they hop and glide.
Chasing shadows, what a race,
Little grapes wearing funny face.

Bursting with life, so full of cheer,
Creating chaos, that's their sphere.
So pop a bunch and join the show,
Grape giggles in the afterglow.

Autumn's Crescendo

In the orchard, giggles grow,
Beneath the boughs where laughter flows.
The squirrels dance in a fruity trance,
Chasing dreams with a silly prance.

Colored leaves make playful hats,
While bees waltz round like fuzzy brats.
Pumpkin-shaped carts roll out in glee,
As the harvest shouts, "Look at me!"

With every crunch, the humor bursts,
Like juicy tales that quench our thirsts.
The cider's bubbling, fun in a cup,
Come join the jest, let's drink it up!

So raise your glass, let's make a toast,
To autumn's feast, we love the most!
With laughter ripe, and joy in the air,
The fall parade is beyond compare!

Drops of Paradise

On sunny days, the world's a dream,
Juicy wonders burst at the seam.
Each bead of dew shines like a gem,
As giggling raindrops join the hem.

The fruits of joy swing on their vines,
As nature weaves mischievous signs.
With every splash, a joke unfurls,
A comic strip of dancing pearls.

Cherries laugh as they tumble down,
While oranges sport a silly crown.
In the garden, every giggle grows,
Turned into jam, that's how it goes!

So if you seek a tasty jest,
Look to the fruits, they're surely the best.
With every bite, let laughter flow,
In drops of joy, let's steal the show!

Glistening Surprises

Beneath the sun, the colors play,
With fruity puns in bright array.
The watermelons wear their stripes,
While pears sing songs with fruity gripes.

Each cluster glows, a treasure chest,
Where peachy laughs are truly blessed.
The plums are pranking all around,
As cherries gather, joy unbound.

With giggles stuffed in every bite,
The snacks delight from morn till night.
A fruit fiesta for the brave,
In every taste, the fun we crave!

So let's not fret over silly things,
When life gives us fruit, let laughter ring.
With every crunch, surprises bloom,
Glistening smiles erase the gloom!

Green and Gold Portraits

In leafy realms where giggles sprout,
The green and gold dance all about.
Avocados cracking wise on trees,
While lemons laugh with cheeky breeze.

The zest of life reflects the sun,
Each fruit rejoices, oh what fun!
With nature's palette, bright and bold,
These portraits tell of laughter untold.

In every harvest, a prank unfolds,
Beans wear hats made of marigolds.
Pickles ponder in a game of chess,
Making life a briny mess!

So gather round, let's have a feast,
With veggies ripe, our laughter increased.
For in this garden, funny and bright,
Each bite's a joke, each taste a delight!

Beneath the Lush Canopy

Underneath leaves, I take a seat,
A bunch of friends, none can be beat.
We giggle and sway with the gentle breeze,
As laughter dances through rows of trees.

The sun spills juice on our silly hats,
We toast with fruit juice, as fun chitchats.
Mischievous squirrels join in our game,
Pretending they're noble, all the same.

The vines are tangled with playful cheer,
Reaching for dreams, not a hint of fear.
Each grape a story, each laugh a delight,
Under the canopy, we dance through the night.

So swing from a branch, let worries flee,
In this grape-filled realm, where we're all free.
Creating our world, one giggle at a time,
Woven together, like this silly rhyme.

Vine-Kissed Dreams

In a field where the fuzzy grapes grow,
We daydream of juice and a crazy show.
A parade of flavors, oh what a sight,
Dancing like grapes on a hot summer night.

The vines whisper jokes in a green-fingered way,
While we laugh and munch, turning worries to play.
A grape wearing glasses gets the biggest cheer,
As we roll on the grass, the world feels so near.

The sun on our faces, sweet juices do flow,
We giggle at grapes, each one making us glow.
Winged friends join in, flapping all around,
Adding to the fun in our vine-kissed playground.

With each squished grape, new jokes will arise,
So come, let's create, under wide-open skies.
In the land of the vine, where laughter is prime,
We'll bottle our joy, one grape at a time.

Juices of Autumn

Autumn comes in with a colorful splash,
Grapes giggle loudly, none make a dash.
They bounce in their baskets like kids on the street,
Enjoying the fun of their ripe little feat.

The leaves wear their gold like a prideful crown,
While we munch juicy snacks, never a frown.
A hiccup from soda makes everyone laugh,
As we sip and we stumble, take shots by the half.

Grapevine karaoke fills the air with our cheer,
The grapes croon out tunes, oh so loud and clear.
With each fruity note, melodies so grand,
We prance in the fields, hand in hand.

So gather your friends, as autumn rolls near,
For laughter and juice, let's raise a loud cheer.
We'll dance through the orchards, revel and play,
Autumn's sweet laughter marks each fruitful day.

The Orchard's Whisper

In the orchard where whispers tickle the vines,
Grapes share their gossip, with giggly designs.
An apple's a joker, wears a dandy hat,
While pears make puns about leaving their spats.

The sun tickles leaves, makes shadows that dance,
With grapes telling secrets, we join in the prance.
A dance-off erupts, but grapes start to slip,
Rolling downhill, like a fruity old trip.

Here in the orchard, we brainstorm ideas,
Like bottled-up giggles, they flow through the years.
Every spry little bud blooms into a jest,
As friends weave together that which we love best.

So gather your crew, let laughter ensue,
In this giggling patch, there's room for your crew.
Embrace all the chaos, let joy take its place,
In the orchard's brisk air, we'll all find our grace.

A Cluster of Joy

Beneath the vine, we laugh and play,
Our worries tossed, they slip away.
With grape-stained hands, we dance around,
In fruit-filled fun, our joy is found.

Unruly bunches, tumbling down,
Like silly clowns in purple gowns.
We chase the rolls with fruity cheer,
Who knew the grapes could bring such beer?

In shades of green and purple gloom,
We light the night with laughter's bloom.
Each bite a giggle, a juice-splashed spree,
Our merry hearts, as light as can be.

So come and join this crazy vine,
As juicy laughs and bursts combine.
In every drop, our humor's spry,
A cluster of joy, oh me, oh my!

Vine-Woven Dreams

In tangled vines, we weave our schemes,
With grape-filled jests and fruit-filled dreams.
We swing from leaves, oh what a sight,
Like acrobats on a juicy night.

The wine flows free, our voices high,
Each sip's a joke, we laugh and sigh.
From grape to glass, a winding road,
What funny tales our juice can load!

We stomp and squish, our feet parade,
With giggles that never seem to fade.
A fruity riddle, a punchline sweet,
As laughter dances on our feet.

So raise your grapes and toast your dreams,
In vineyard vines, or so it seems.
With jokes entwined, our spirits beam,
In this vine-woven world of gleam.

Candied Melodies

A plump delight, our voices rise,
With candies tossed, we're in a size.
Each grape a note, a tune so fine,
We sing of joy, like sugar wine.

Bouncing grapes and giggles sway,
In candied rhythms, come what may.
We play the fields, we twirl around,
With laughter bursting from the ground.

Each melody becomes a snack,
As grape juice runs from front to back.
The tunes we hum, a fruity jam,
Mixing our laughter as best we can.

In candied dreams, we find our place,
In folly's grip, a playful chase.
So join this song, let laughter soar,
With melodies, we can't ignore!

Juicy Promises of Tomorrow

Grapes tumble down, our futures bright,
With laughter's promise, a pure delight.
For every squish, a dream unfurled,
Juicy futures in a zany world.

We chase the sun and dance in shade,
With fruity hopes that never fade.
Giggles pop like bubbles in air,
In juicy whispers, oh, we dare!

A grape for every silly thought,
In this parade of cheer we've caught.
We toast to tomorrow, ripe and bold,
With laughter's tales, forever told.

So grab a bunch, come join the race,
In every laugh, a sweet embrace.
With juicy promises, we will sing,
As joy's our harvest, let it spring!

Threads of Harvest

In the field, I prance with glee,
A bunch of fruit calls out to me.
I trip on vines, oh what a sight,
Grapes roll around, a comical flight.

Squished and squashed, we dance and play,
Nature's jellybean, hip-hip-hooray!
With every tumble, laughter flows,
A juicy mess, but who really knows?

My friends join in, the fun's begun,
With grape mustaches, we're second to none.
We toast with juice, a cheerful cheer,
Who knew harvest could bring such cheer?

So here's a wink to our silly spree,
With all this fruit, we're wild and free.
Let's add some giggles to our feasts,
In the land of grapes, we are the beasts!

Garden Serenade

In the garden, laughter grows,
Poking our heads, like garden gnomes.
The grapes are swaying, all in a line,
They whisper jokes about the sunshine.

I tell a tale of a grape's grand dream,
To roll in the mud, oh how they gleam!
With every squirt, we giggle loud,
Join the ruckus, let's make a crowd!

A crafty squirrel boasting its heist,
Stole my lunch, oh what a slice!
But grapes just chuckle, they've seen it all,
Their juicy giggles, a fruity brawl.

So strut through the vines, let's twirl and sway,
With grapes as our friends, we'll dance today.
Their plump little skins can handle the fun,
In this garden we've made, we've already won!

The Joy of Yield

Harvest time, what a silly sight,
Baskets full, oh what delight!
I wield my scissors, snip, snip, snip,
Grapes tumble down, take a flying trip!

One bounced high and hit a bee,
That fuzzy fellow buzzed angrily!
But grapes just laughed, no worries here,
Their giggles echo, loud and clear.

A grape on my shoulder, a wine glass hat,
The party's on, can you imagine that?
With juice in our cups, we toast the night,
Sipping and laughing, a glorious sight!

So raise your goblet, join the parade,
In this joyous mess, adventures are made.
With every sip of mishap and cheer,
We cherish the harvest, year after year!

Essence of Eden

In Eden's realm, a playful jest,
Grapes giggle softly, they're truly blessed.
They peek from leaves, in search of a spy,
"Can't catch us now!" they laugh and fly.

A fruit bowl race, oh what a roar,
Grapes rolling first, I'd open the door.
Orange and apple, tried to keep pace,
But those sneaky grapes won the whole race!

With fruity banter, secrets they share,
"Who's got the juice? It's only fair!"
A squished little grape, said, "Don't despair,
We spill the fun, it's in the air!"

So cackle and giggle, in this Eden land,
With rolling grapes, oh isn't it grand?
Let laughter be the sweetest embrace,
In the vine-meadow wild, we'll find our place!

The Taste of Afternoon

The sun beams down, a golden light,
While ducks in shades of green take flight.
My fingers sticky from fruit so round,
Laughter echoes, joy is found.

My teeth sink deep, the juice flows free,
A sticky grin, who will save me?
Friends giggle as the juice does drip,
We're all aboard this flavor trip.

But ants march in, a tiny parade,
With tiny backpacks, they can't evade.
A feast for us, a feast for pests,
Our picnic turns into their quests.

So here we munch, our voices loud,
While crafty ants just feel so proud.
A fruity mess, a sunny show,
In nature's laugh, we feel the glow.

Portrait of a Vineyard

A canvas lush with colors bright,
Where bunches hang with sheer delight.
Each cluster laughing, playing dress,
A grapey giggle, who would guess?

The leaves are dancing, breezy cheer,
While bunnies hop, they have no fear.
With hats adorned, they stop to stare,
At the wearers who stop to share.

A silly painter, what a sight,
Splatters purple; oh, what a fright!
A brush of chaos, joy unleashed,
Leaving us craving, at least a feast.

The grapes pretend to glisten wide,
A merry prank, they won't abide.
For every bite, a laugh does grow,
In this sweet chaos, spirits flow.

Liquid Sunbeams

In a glass of gold, a summer's kiss,
A splash of laughter, oh, what bliss!
Each sip is like a wobbly dance,
Makes you giggle, puts you in a trance.

A fountain of joy, it spills and sways,
As friends erupt in silly praise.
With silly straws, we toast so bright,
To sips of sunshine, pure delight!

But oh dear me, what's that we see?
A fruit fly buzzing, oh so free!
He takes a leap, a daring dive,
Crashing our party, just to thrive.

We sip in jest, with wide-eyed cheers,
As fruit flies fly, quenching our fears.
A toast to laughter, to every drop,
In liquid sunbeams, we never stop!

Embrace of the Seasons

A grapevine sways in breezy air,
Each season's dance, a lively affair.
With winter's chill, they snuggle tight,
While summer bursts, oh what a sight!

Autumn's hug, a spiced embrace,
As leaves swirl down, a joyful race.
While grapes play hide and seek inside,
In every nook, their joys abide.

Spring brings pranks, a froggy choir,
With nature's giggles, never tire.
The sun gives chase, a playful tease,
As grapeful moments drift on breeze.

So here we stand, through every turn,
In seasons' laughter, we brightly yearn.
For each grape's tale, so full of cheer,
In nature's waltz, we hold it dear.

Fruity Lullabies

In twilight's glow, the fruits convene,
Chanting tunes with a juicy sheen.
Bouncing berries full of cheer,
Whispering secrets only they hear.

The peaches giggle, rolling down,
While bananas wear a silly frown.
Oranges dance in circles wide,
Melons waddle, oh what a ride!

A grape slips by with a smug little grin,
Saying, "Who needs a violin?"
While cherries play tag, don't you know,
Hiding behind a leafy bow!

As night falls soft, the laughter grows,
In fruity dreams, anything goes.
So close your eyes, dream of the feast,
Tomorrow awaits—a juicy beast!

The Garden's Secret Kiss

In the garden where giggles grow,
Wink of a flower, putting on a show.
Berries blush in a sunlit blush,
Fruits whisper tales in a gentle hush.

The carrots chuckle, arms akimbo,
As cabbages boast with a proud lingo.
Tomatoes blushing in their red attire,
Beans leap high, fueled by desire.

The corn stalks sway, playing it cool,
While squash rides by on a noodle-duel.
"Let's hold hands," cried the cucumbers bright,
Shattering silence and bringing delight.

A cheeky beet gives a flirtatious pout,
In this garden, fun never runs out.
As the moon grins with a silvery kiss,
Fruits and veggies spin in bliss!

A Symphony of Ripeness

In orchards bright, a band takes stage,
Conducted by nature, it's all the rage.
The apples strum their shiny red skin,
While grapes break out in a joyful spin.

The bananas hum in perfect tune,
Underneath the watchful moon.
Pineapples all dressed in gold,
Bouncing to rhythms brave and bold.

Melons roll in a cheerful spree,
Flavored notes of harmony.
Cherries clap with a cherry chime,
While figs keep perfect time!

With laughter loud, the fruits unite,
In this fruity symphony, sheer delight.
So join the dance, let worries be,
Sway with the music, wild and free!

Serene Sips of Summer

A pitcher pours with a cheerful clink,
Fruits swirling in a rosy pink.
Lemon laughs with a zestful twist,
While mint sneaks in; it can't be missed.

The berries tumble, making quite a splash,
Creating chaos in a jolly mash.
Kiwi slides on a slippery ride,
As laughter bubbles, oh what a tide!

Ice cubes cheer in a clinky race,
Chilling drinks in this silly place.
Each sip a giggle, refreshing and bright,
In sunny delight, what a fine sight!

With every gulp, joy takes a stand,
In this summer's cup, oh isn't life grand?
Raise your glass to the flavors we cheer,
In every drop, bring friends near!

Hidden Treasures in the Canopy

High up in the leaves, such a sight to see,
Tiny critters playing, living wild and free.
A squirrel with a stash, thinks he's quite the lord,
Grinning at a bird, saying, 'Who needs a hoard?'

Light filters in, a spotlight on the show,
Where acorns are currency, just watch them grow.
A dance of shadows, in the tree's embrace,
Nature's little secrets, can't keep up the pace.

Ripe Reflections of Serenity

In the pond's still glass, a frog starts to muse,
'Why is everyone here? Got better things to choose!'
He leaps with a splash, causing ripples galore,
While ducks just quack back, 'You're not keeping score!'

Reflections of laughter, floating on the breeze,
A dance of the reeds, swaying with such ease.
Cattails offer gossip, they whisper and sway,
While fish flip and flop, 'Look at us display!'

The Dance of Autumn Colors

Leaves twirl like dancers, putting on a show,
Yellow, red, and orange, their final tableau.
A breeze gives a chuckle, nudging them around,
'Who's losing the battle? Fall's calling your sound!'

Squirrels scamper quick, collecting their sticks,
'This whole thing's a circus, come join in the mix!'
Pumpkins roll with laughter, round and full of glee,
'Who needs a trick-or-treat? Just feast on me!'

Garden Alchemy

In the garden of whimsy, magic starts to bloom,
Where tomatoes have legs, running 'round with a zoom.
'Watch out for the carrots!' they yell with delight,
'They'll blend up a potion, if you don't hold tight!'

Herbs gossip softly, in the warm, sunny glow,
'What's the latest news? We've got a tasty show!'
Bees wear tiny hats, buzzing with such flair,
In this patch of laughter, no worries, no care.

www.ingramcontent.com/pod-product-compliance
Lightning Source LLC
Chambersburg PA
CBHW060126230426
43661CB00003B/345